Revealing You
A Journal for Birthmothers

Michelle Thorne

To Charles Payton,
with love.
Thank you for modeling intimacy with Abba.

www.michellethornebooks.com

TABLE OF CONTENTS

PREFACE

1. NEW NORMAL

2. BLACK, WHITE AND GREY

3. DEALING WITH THESE PEOPLE

4. TALKING TO YOUR KIDS ABOUT BEING A BIRTHMOTHER

5. FORGIVENESS

6. CONTINUING IN LOVE

7. WORTHY TO BE KNOWN

8. LETTING GO

9. BIRTHDAYS

10. HOLIDAYS

11. CHRISTMAS

12. YOUR STORY

13. MOVING FROM GRIEF TO CELEBRATION

14. 20 QUESTIONS

"I can't go back to yesterday because I was a different person then."

— Lewis Carroll, *Alice in Wonderland*

"The great thing to remember is that though our feelings come and go God's love for us does not."

—**C.S. Lewis**

PREFACE

This journal is for birthmoms from a birthmom. I am a birthmom, and you are my people. Let me tell you, my love for you is big. So, so big!

I am also a Pregnancy Counselor. I have seen a need for a journal for women post-placement—a workbook, if you will—to tell these amazing stories and get some of the feelings out. But the trouble is you don't know what you don't know. It's hard to begin to get things out when there is so much to get out. It's hard to commit to a feeling when there are so many. Which one is the right one?

The grief alone is paralyzing. It is completely overwhelming, right? I know it. I know it well, friend.

In John Green's heart-breaking book, *The Fault in Our Stars*, Hazel has a conversation with Peter Van Houten after the death of her beloved Gus. Van Houten makes this remarkable comment. He says, "Grief does not change you, Hazel. It reveals you." Your journey through adoption post-placement will reveal you. It will give you choices. It will be honest, even if you're not.

"The great thing to remember is that though our feelings come and go God's love for us does not."
—C.S. Lewis

When I placed my son in March of 2000, I did nothing but unabashedly bawl my eyes out and write for weeks. I had to get it out, but I had no direction. It was tender and painful, and almost impossible to touch, like an abscess deep in my heart. I was crazy with depression and I couldn't talk about it.

I was supposed to be "better" since I "did the right thing" for my son. No pressure there to fit in a box and make others more comfortable with my story than I was myself. Nope. No manipulation either. Not a bit!

Needless to say, I needed help. I didn't know any other birthmothers who lived near me. Nobody got it. I wasn't even sure I got it yet. Writing in a journal saved me. It gave my grief an outlet, let me be completely honest without fear, and allowed me to ask questions that were scary. I hope you find the same freedom here.

I created this journal using a gray scale. I did this on purpose. First, this stuff isn't pretty. There are parts that are dark and nasty and there are parts that are pure and light. So, I needed the contrast. Second, I didn't want to color any of your pages. I wanted you to choose and respond however you see fit. Different colors of ink can mean different things to you. Crayons in the margins, stamps in the corners, watercolors across the page—this journal is blank so you can fill it. Fill it with whatever you want to. Paste pictures inside of it, draw, and/or write poetry. There were days in my journal when I could only manage one word—help. You have the freedom to do as much or as little as you can/want. Do whatever helps you.

This journal is for you alone. You don't have to go in order. You don't have to do every chapter. You don't have to like what I say. You can follow along and use the prompts as a guide, or you can mark over every word I wrote and swear, though swearing will only get you so far. Either way, get it out. Name it. Name the thing. Name the pain. Name the offense. Name the anger. Cry out to God. Cry out loud. Cry out on paper. Cry out. Cry.

It is a process. God loves process; we hate it. This journal will hold your hand and lead you through the process of grieving and healing, as it relates to being a birthmother. This journal is not all inclusive. As every adoption is as unique as the individuals in them, you may not feel that some of this applies to you. You may have to alter the language. You may have to do more work with a counselor or support group. That's okay! Take courage, friend. Your story isn't over yet, and you are not alone!

"The great thing to remember is that though our feelings come and go God's love for us does not."
—**C.S. Lewis**

"The great thing to remember is that though our feelings come and go God's love for us does not."

—**C.S. Lewis**

"Numbing the pain for a while will make it worse when you finally feel it."

— J.K. Rowling, *Harry Potter and the Goblet of Fire*

Grief can make you feel like youre on an island, but it doesnt have to be that way. The grief experiences of others can make you feel less alone, heard, & seen. Leaning on God & His people can transform a dark-night-of-the-soul kind of experience into a beautiful display of God's love & grace.

1

NEW NORMAL

Birthmother. The title now applies to you, but what does that mean exactly? How do you wade through the rough waters of placing a child for adoption? A birthmother, is a woman who gave birth to a child and for whatever reason chose to place that child for adoption. That is you. You are a birthmother.

There is a new normal to get used to, right? At first, you were consumed with the birth process and time in the hospital. But that walk out of the hospital, the one that has been described as the longest walk ever taken, it was rough. Now, you are at home with a new normal.

> New Normal=The current state of being after some dramatic change has transpired. What replaces the expected, usual, typical state after an event occurs. The new normal encourages one to deal with current situations rather than lamenting what could have been. (Urban Dictionary)

How do you make sense of this life when everything is the same but you? You have experienced a major life event. You have had a baby! Whether this child was celebrated or ignored by your loved ones, it was a major event for you. To add to that, you have placed that baby (i.e. suffered the loss of a child). Even if you have an open adoption, placing a child for adoption is a loss.

This moment, this is the one you realize that your adoption experience is both/and. There is joy and pain. There are moments to celebrate and moments to grieve. And let's just start there.

"The great thing to remember is that though our feelings come and go God's love for us does not."
—C.S. Lewis

Stop and acknowledge your moments. **What makes your heart so full you feel it might burst? When do you feel such love that you can't contain it? What parts are hard to think about? What moments make you feel hollow or angry?**

They are all there, right? Your experience in having a baby and placing him/her for adoption is both/and. That is normal, and it is good to know. You can acknowledge both.

Jesus had both/and. He experienced unfathomable joy and deep sorrow. Jesus' story includes highs and lows, to put it mildly. This story of yours can be and will be both. I encourage you to have and to hold both of them.

So, take time now to write out your birth story. It can be long or short, detailed or sparse. You can start anywhere you want. Recount what physically happened. Where were you when you went into labor? What happened then? When was this? How long did you labor? Who is this new little person in your life? When was he/she born? What did they look like? What are the details of your baby's birth? Name? Date? Time? Who, if anyone, was with you? Did you hold your baby? Did your baby stay with you in your room or somewhere else? How did you feel physically after delivery? How did you feel emotionally? Did you feed, change, and/or rock your baby?

The days after delivery are hard. They just are. You think once you have the baby you will begin to move forward, but really, you are just beginning. So much has changed. So much is still the same. It's a strange juxtaposition of the life you were living and the new you. A lot of times, you don't quite fit into that old way any more, even if your behaviors haven't changed, your life has.

This is a blessing. Something new is happening.

Isaiah 43:18-19 (NASB)
Do not call to mind the former things,
Or ponder things of the past.

"The great thing to remember is that though our feelings come and go God's love for us does not."
—**C.S. Lewis**

Behold, I will do something new,
Now it will spring forth;
Will you not be aware of it?
I will even make a roadway in the wilderness,
Rivers in the desert.

What is your new normal? How have you transitioned into your life post-placement? What has surprised you about your life after placement? What things of the past have you let go? What things of the past do you need to let go? What is the new thing God is doing in you right now?

"The great thing to remember is that though our feelings come and go God's love for us does not."
—C.S. Lewis

"The great thing to remember is that though our feelings come and go God's love for us does not."

—C.S. Lewis

"The great thing to remember is that though our feelings come and go God's love for us does not."
—C.S. Lewis

"The great thing to remember is that though our feelings come and go God's love for us does not."

—C.S. Lewis

"The great thing to remember is that though our feelings come and go God's love for us does not."
—**C.S. Lewis**

"The great thing to remember is that though our feelings come and go God's love for us does not."

—C.S. Lewis

"The great thing to remember is that though our feelings come and go God's love for us does not."

—C.S. Lewis

"The great thing to remember is that though our feelings come and go God's love for us does not."
—C.S. Lewis

_____

_____

_____

_____

_____

_____

_____

_____

_____

_____

_____

_____

_____

_____

_____

_____

_____

_____

_____

_____

"The great thing to remember is that though our feelings come and go God's love for us does not."

—C.S. Lewis

"The great thing to remember is that though our feelings come and go God's love for us does not."

—**C.S. Lewis**

"The great thing to remember is that though our feelings come and go God's love for us does not."

—**C.S. Lewis**

"The great thing to remember is that though our feelings come and go God's love for us does not."
—C.S. Lewis

"The great thing to remember is that though our feelings come and go God's love for us does not."
—**C.S. Lewis**

"The great thing to remember is that though our feelings come and go God's love for us does not."

—C.S. Lewis

"The great thing to remember is that though our feelings come and go God's love for us does not."

—**C.S. Lewis**

"The great thing to remember is that though our feelings come and go God's love for us does not."

—C.S. Lewis

"The great thing to remember is that though our feelings come and go God's love for us does not."

—C.S. Lewis

My adoption journey is messy.
Somedays it's a work of preschool art
and only requires a quick hand washing at the sink to clean up;
somedays it's blood and guts on the highway pavement after a crash
and requires a pressure washer.

"The great thing to remember is that though our feelings come and go God's love for us does not."
—C.S. Lewis

2

BLACK, WHITE AND GREY

There are two sides to every story, and two sides to your story, but it doesn't feel complete. There is a black and white story, positive and negative, and yet, there is still gray. If the black and white are what physically happened, the gray represents the emotions involved.

These parts of the story are harder. They are harder to talk about and harder to heal. These take time because we cannot tangibly take hold of them and rehabilitate them like our physical muscles. However, we can revisit them and work out our *emotional* muscles.

This may sound scary. That's an emotion. So, don't try to avoid feeling scared about it. Instead, ask yourself. Why am I scared? What am I afraid will happen, or not happen, if I reconnect myself to the emotions of placing my child for adoption?

The answer could be anything. There is no right or wrong and the answer may fluctuate. You may feel one way now and differently next week. It may be in the same day. Some days are just harder than others.

If you are going to look at the emotions of your story, you have to look at your story. Go back to the previous section and re-read what you have written about your story. Then, answer these questions.

How did you feel when you found out you were pregnant? Did you smile when you talked about your pregnancy? Are you ashamed of your pregnancy? Are you proud of your child? At what point did you feel angriest/happiest?

"The great thing to remember is that though our feelings come and go God's love for us does not."

—C.S. Lewis

These moments and the awareness of how you feel during them will help you heal. It can be hard to admit. Some people may even call your child a mistake. Your child is not, but the way others treat you and your pregnancy can affect how you feel about it and how you feel about your child.

Take stock of your experience so far. Do you feel free to express yourself and your feelings about your adoption journey? What is holding you back from that? Know that this is a safe place for you to do just that. You can express your deepest most secret feelings here. You are only as sick as your secrets. I don't want you to be sick anymore, friend. I want you to be free, that includes emotional freedom. If you continue to be weighed down by guilt and shame, I have to say that you can stand firm, not in yourself, but in the person of Christ, who took on your guilt and shame and forgave you on the Cross.

I know it is hard. I know it is. The emotional roller coaster is nauseating and controlling and it would have you sit strapped into that moving car for the rest of your life. But friend, I want to encourage you to get off. Get off the roller coaster and stand on solid ground. Stand on the Rock.

How though? How do you get off the emotional roller coaster? Perhaps you begin to recognize that these emotions are important and need to get out, but that they do not determine truth in your life. These emotions don't get to debilitate you. There is something other. There is something more.

Just like when you break a leg, you use crutches to help you walk. You can use this journal to help you feel. A broken leg is just broken. It doesn't make you crippled. The rest of your body doesn't shut down because of it. Stand firm, friend, and don't let these sharp emotions enslave you. Be broken, not crippled.

Galatians 5:1 (NASB)
It was for freedom that Christ set us free; therefore keep standing firm and do not be subject again to a yoke of slavery.

How are you continuing to process your adoption? Have you explored your feelings about your pregnancy and placement? How did you feel at first? How did you feel at birth? How do you feel now? Do your emotions control you at times? How do you cope emotionally? Do you carry any guilt about your pregnancy? What needs to change for you to feel and function simultaneously?

"The great thing to remember is that though our feelings come and go God's love for us does not."
—C.S. Lewis

"The great thing to remember is that though our feelings come and go God's love for us does not."
—C.S. Lewis

"The great thing to remember is that though our feelings come and go God's love for us does not."
—**C.S. Lewis**

"The great thing to remember is that though our feelings come and go God's love for us does not."
—**C.S. Lewis**

"The great thing to remember is that though our feelings come and go God's love for us does not."
—**C.S. Lewis**

"The great thing to remember is that though our feelings come and go God's love for us does not."
—**C.S. Lewis**

"The great thing to remember is that though our feelings come and go God's love for us does not."
—**C.S. Lewis**

"The great thing to remember is that though our feelings come and go God's love for us does not."
—C.S. Lewis

"The great thing to remember is that though our feelings come and go God's love for us does not."
—C.S. Lewis

"The great thing to remember is that though our feelings come and go God's love for us does not."

—**C.S. Lewis**

"The great thing to remember is that though our feelings come and go God's love for us does not."

—C.S. Lewis

"The great thing to remember is that though our feelings come and go God's love for us does not."
—C.S. Lewis

"The great thing to remember is that though our feelings come and go God's love for us does not."

—**C.S. Lewis**

"The great thing to remember is that though our feelings come and go God's love for us does not."

—C.S. Lewis

"The great thing to remember is that though our feelings come and go God's love for us does not."

—C.S. Lewis

"The friend who can be silent with us in a moment of despair or confusion, who can stay with us in an hour of grief and bereavement, who can tolerate not knowing... not healing, not curing... that is a friend who cares."

— Henri Nouwen

"The great thing to remember is that though our feelings come and go God's love for us does not."
—C.S. Lewis

3

DEALING WITH THESE PEOPLE

In your new normal, everyone else is just who they were before. And you? Not even close. You may feel very alone. Even if you had strong support from your family, they still will not "get it" the way another birthmother will.

I want to offer you some freedom here. That is okay. It's okay if they don't get it and it's okay if you feel differently about it than they do. Everyone will feel differently. Your parents are at a different life-stage than you are. Your siblings are different people than you are. Your children may or may not be old enough to handle what just happened. All of this is part of your new normal and that does not make it bad, it just makes it real.

You may not know now (spoiler alert!), but you will soon find out that adoption is a train you don't get off of. You are on the Birthmother Train now. The rest of your life, birthmother will be a title you carry. Throughout your life others will see your experience and your choice differently than you do. That's okay. Part of what I have learned as a birthmother is that I am allowed to be where I am without permission or apology, and in turn, others are allowed to be where they are without permission or apology. I can only control myself.

So when you get that rude comment or that ugly message on social media, you don't have to let it ruin you. It will inform you. This kind of big girl decision will reveal to you who people are. The way others respond will inform you of your crowd.

"The great thing to remember is that though our feelings come and go God's love for us does not."
—C.S. Lewis

From this point on in your life, I give you permission (if you need it) to walk out of relationships that are harmful to you. You don't have to be gone forever, but you do need to leave.

There are people and relationships I have had to let go of and grieve in my life because of my adoption story. Leaving was good for me. Until I could be in the same 'space' with the other person and not feel less than, I had to stay gone. You want to know what I found out from doing that? I didn't need them in the first place.

So many times I looked to others to legitimate my thoughts, my goals, my identity. No one, you hear me, no one can do that for you except Jesus. I don't know how you feel about Him, but it's true. And honestly, I don't think He wants us around people who are poisonous to us. He is on your team. He is for you every time, all the time.

Dealing with these people means dealing with yourself first. You have a child now. You don't have room or time for toxic relationships. This child, who you undoubtedly love with every fiber of your being, is a sponge. In your time with him/her, in your correspondence, what are they soaking up? What do you want them to soak up? How are you modeling honesty and health for them now? What needs to change?

Learning to articulate your story and how you feel, being willing to say 'no' and step away, and advocating for yourself in your life will come. First, be you. Learn you and be you. You are worth it!

Do you have people in your life that feel differently than you do about your choice to place your child? Who are they? What are some things they have said that have made it easy/hard for you? Who are you angry with? Why? Who are you afraid to talk to? Why? Who do you need to leave? Why? Who are you? What is most like you to do? What are some of your favorites? Are you enjoying you? What do you want to learn about yourself?

Start now by acknowledging these things and ask God to help you walk in freedom and forgiveness. Write to God on the following pages. Pour your heart out to Him. It doesn't have to make sense or be grammatically correct. Just be you, right now, where you are.

"The great thing to remember is that though our feelings come and go God's love for us does not."
—C.S. Lewis

"The great thing to remember is that though our feelings come and go God's love for us does not."
—**C.S. Lewis**

"The great thing to remember is that though our feelings come and go God's love for us does not."

—**C.S. Lewis**

"The great thing to remember is that though our feelings come and go God's love for us does not."
—**C.S. Lewis**

"The great thing to remember is that though our feelings come and go God's love for us does not."

—C.S. Lewis

"The great thing to remember is that though our feelings come and go God's love for us does not."

—C.S. Lewis

"The great thing to remember is that though our feelings come and go God's love for us does not."

—**C.S. Lewis**

"The great thing to remember is that though our feelings come and go God's love for us does not."
—C.S. Lewis

"The great thing to remember is that though our feelings come and go God's love for us does not."

—**C.S. Lewis**

_____

_____

_____

_____

_____

_____

_____

_____

_____

_____

_____

_____

_____

_____

_____

_____

_____

_____

_____

_____

_____

_____

"The great thing to remember is that though our feelings come and go God's love for us does not."

—C.S. Lewis

_____

_____

_____

_____

_____

_____

_____

_____

_____

_____

_____

_____

_____

_____

_____

_____

_____

_____

_____

"The great thing to remember is that though our feelings come and go God's love for us does not."

—C.S. Lewis

"The great thing to remember is that though our feelings come and go God's love for us does not."

—C.S. Lewis

"The great thing to remember is that though our feelings come and go God's love for us does not."

—**C.S. Lewis**

"The great thing to remember is that though our feelings come and go God's love for us does not."
—**C.S. Lewis**

"The great thing to remember is that though our feelings come and go God's love for us does not."
—**C.S. Lewis**

"The great thing to remember is that though our feelings come and go God's love for us does not."

—C.S. Lewis

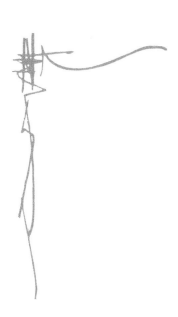

"Yes, Mother. I can see you are flawed. You have not hidden it. That is your greatest gift to me."

— Alice Walker

4

TALKING TO YOUR KIDS ABOUT BEING A BIRTHMOTHER

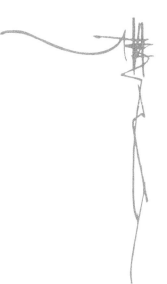

How do you do it? Early, often and full of grace. Talking to your children about placement is hard to do. You have to own your mistakes. You have to forgive yourself. You have to know that they may say things that hurt and your children might hurt because of your choice. It is hard.

I encourage you to let them in. Let them know that you made a choice that is still affecting you and now affecting them. Let them know you are not perfect and that's okay. Show them you can love yourself and the child you placed. Be their model.

2 Corinthians 4:2-4 (NIV)
Rather, we have renounced secret and shameful ways; we do not use deception, nor do we distort the word of God. On the contrary, by setting forth the truth plainly we commend ourselves to everyone's conscience in the sight of God.

One thing that will help you is to know who you are, to have a solid sense of your identity. You need to know, or begin to discover, that your whole identity is not as a birthmother. Even if you do not have other children yet, it is good to have an accurate sense of self.

Being a birthmother is only part of who you are. It is an imprint. An imprint is a lasting mark made by pressure. It is something that happens to a larger whole.

You, beautiful you, have an imprint but there is more to you. When you know this, you can begin to talk about your experience and answer rude/hard/ignorant questions about your choice to place your child for adoption.

"The great thing to remember is that though our feelings come and go God's love for us does not."
—C.S. Lewis

I placed my first child for adoption. Later, when I had more children, I was lost and scared. How am I going to tell my other children about my first child? My husband suggested that I start with our daughter as an infant. "Just go in there and hold her and tell her the story. Tell her about him." That really worked for me. Then, when my son came along, I was practiced. Now, as they continue to grow and have questions, I don't go into a major panic and we don't have to do the work of laying the foundation every time.

Also, I wanted my son's adoptive parents to tell him from the beginning that he is adopted. I wanted adoption to be part of his normal life. It is the same with the children I am parenting. They have a brother that is part of their normal, though he does not live with us. Adoption is part of their normal as well.

How can you begin, or prepare yourself, to talk to your children about your adoption journey? What is the simplest way for you to begin? What creative way can you involve them? What will you do when you don't know an answer to a question? What will you do when you don't want to answer? How can you honor your children's curiosity when the questions are difficult to answer?

"The great thing to remember is that though our feelings come and go God's love for us does not."

—**C.S. Lewis**

"The great thing to remember is that though our feelings come and go God's love for us does not."
—C.S. Lewis

"The great thing to remember is that though our feelings come and go God's love for us does not."
—C.S. Lewis

"The great thing to remember is that though our feelings come and go God's love for us does not."

—C.S. Lewis

"The great thing to remember is that though our feelings come and go God's love for us does not."

—C.S. Lewis

"The great thing to remember is that though our feelings come and go God's love for us does not."

—C.S. Lewis

"The great thing to remember is that though our feelings come and go God's love for us does not."

—C.S. Lewis

"The great thing to remember is that though our feelings come and go God's love for us does not."
—**C.S. Lewis**

"The great thing to remember is that though our feelings come and go God's love for us does not."

—C.S. Lewis

"The great thing to remember is that though our feelings come and go God's love for us does not."
—**C.S. Lewis**

"The great thing to remember is that though our feelings come and go God's love for us does not."
—C.S. Lewis

"The great thing to remember is that though our feelings come and go God's love for us does not."
—**C.S. Lewis**

"The great thing to remember is that though our feelings come and go God's love for us does not."

—C.S. Lewis

"The great thing to remember is that though our feelings come and go God's love for us does not."
—**C.S. Lewis**

"The great thing to remember is that though our feelings come and go God's love for us does not."
—**C.S. Lewis**

"The great thing to remember is that though our feelings come and go God's love for us does not."

—C.S. Lewis

"You can't forgive without loving. And I don't mean sentimentality. I don't mean mush. I mean having enough courage to stand up and say, 'I forgive. I'm finished with it.'"

— Maya Angelou

"The rule is: we cannot really forgive ourselves unless we look at the failure in our past and call it by its right name."
— Lewis B. Smedes, *Forgive & Forget: Healing the Hurts*

"The great thing to remember is that though our feelings come and go God's love for us does not."
—C.S. Lewis

5

FORGIVENESS

Why do we forgive? I think Lewis B. Smedes said it best in his book, *The Art of Forgiving*. "To forgive is to set a prisoner free and discover that the prisoner was you." I am intrinsically motivated to forgive because it gives me my freedom.

As a birthmother I have had to forgive people over and over. I have to forgive when loved ones ignore my child's existence and forgive others when they are invasive. I have to forgive the Church for asking me to choose life and judging me while I carried that life to term. I had to realize that God is different than His people and God is different from me. I can't count on Him to respond like my father would, or my mother. He doesn't judge me the way I judge myself.

Perhaps most importantly, I have had to forgive myself. I have to forgive myself for having sex outside of marriage. I have to forgive myself for not being ready. I have to forgive myself for considering abortion. I have to forgive myself for hoping for a miscarriage so I wouldn't be publicly disgraced. I have to forgive myself for partying after I placed. I have to forgive myself for how my decisions affect all my children.

I am the hardest person for me to forgive. What about you? Who is hardest for you to forgive? Why? There is such power in forgiveness. It is a healing balm. If you are holding onto an offense, I hope you will consider letting it go and letting your heart heal.

Here are a couple of Scriptures that talk about forgiveness, but there are so many others.

"The great thing to remember is that though our feelings come and go God's love for us does not."
—C.S. Lewis

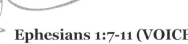

Ephesians 1:7-11 (VOICE)

⁷ *Visualize this:* His blood *freely flowing down the cross,* setting us free! We are forgiven for our sinful ways by the richness of His grace, ⁸ which He has poured all over us. With all wisdom and insight, ⁹ He has enlightened us to the great mystery *at the center* of His will. With immense pleasure, He laid out His intentions *through Jesus,* ¹⁰ a plan that will climax when the time is right *as He returns to create order and unity*—both in heaven and on earth—when all things are brought together under the Anointed's *royal rule.* In Him ¹¹ we stand to inherit even more. As His heirs, we are predestined *to play a key role* in His *unfolding* purpose that is energizing everything to conform to His will.

Ephesians 4:31-32 (VOICE)

³¹ Banish bitterness, rage and anger, shouting and slander, and any and all malicious thoughts—*these are poison.* ³² Instead, be kind and compassionate. *Graciously* forgive one another just as God has forgiven you through the Anointed, *our Liberating King.*

Even when we were still sinners, Christ died for us, the Word says. Christ died for us before we were born, before we asked forgiveness. Christ can help you forgive even if it's hard...Even if the wound inflicted feels impossible to forgive...Even if your offender hasn't apologized. When you forgive, you free yourself. And the truth is, if you are in Christ, **you are already free**. So, walk in that!

As you process, write out the offense, who did it, and how it made you feel. Ask God to take you back 'there' and help you to forgive everyone you need to. Even if there are people you love and it's hard to admit they hurt or offended you, you may need to forgive them. Believe that He will help you.

I challenge you to forgive yourself, forgive the birthfather, forgive your parents, and leave room to forgive them again as the future unfolds. Forgiveness is not static. We must walk in it daily. It is an active process and part of our daily lives.

"The great thing to remember is that though our feelings come and go God's love for us does not."

—C.S. Lewis

"The great thing to remember is that though our feelings come and go God's love for us does not."

—**C.S. Lewis**

"The great thing to remember is that though our feelings come and go God's love for us does not."

—C.S. Lewis

"The great thing to remember is that though our feelings come and go God's love for us does not."
—**C.S. Lewis**

"The great thing to remember is that though our feelings come and go God's love for us does not."
—**C.S. Lewis**

"The great thing to remember is that though our feelings come and go God's love for us does not."
—**C.S. Lewis**

"The great thing to remember is that though our feelings come and go God's love for us does not."

—C.S. Lewis

"The great thing to remember is that though our feelings come and go God's love for us does not."
—C.S. Lewis

"The great thing to remember is that though our feelings come and go God's love for us does not."

—C.S. Lewis

"The great thing to remember is that though our feelings come and go God's love for us does not."

—C.S. Lewis

"The great thing to remember is that though our feelings come and go God's love for us does not."

—**C.S. Lewis**

"The great thing to remember is that though our feelings come and go God's love for us does not."
—**C.S. Lewis**

"The great thing to remember is that though our feelings come and go God's love for us does not."
—**C.S. Lewis**

_____

_____

_____

_____

_____

_____

_____

_____

_____

_____

_____

_____

_____

_____

_____

_____

_____

_____

_____

_____

_____

_____

"The great thing to remember is that though our feelings come and go God's love for us does not."
—C.S. Lewis

"The great thing to remember is that though our feelings come and go God's love for us does not."
—**C.S. Lewis**

"The great thing to remember is that though our feelings come and go God's love for us does not."
—C.S. Lewis

"I must trust that the little bit of love that I sow now will bear many fruits, here in this world and the life to come."

— Henri Nouwen

"The great thing to remember is that though our feelings come and go God's love for us does not."

—C.S. Lewis

6

CONTINUING IN LOVE

1 John 4:19 (NASB)
We love, because He first loved us.

We are not done loving when we place a child for adoption. We continue to love, and not love them as an infant or stick to that *one loving thing* we did, but we love them as they are each day. We continue to love them as they grow. Love brings intimacy. Intimacy can be aptly defined like this: into me see. It means that you reveal your heart, and that can be terrifying. It may mean telling your child hard truths when appropriate, asking his/her forgiveness, and/or smothering him/her with love. Intimacy may mean being available to your child if he/she has questions. It may mean not being a part of your child's life, if that is what your child chooses.

C.S. Lewis said, "Love is not merely affectionate feeling, but a steady wish for the loved person's ultimate good as far as it can be obtained." I love this quote because it focuses on the Loved not the Lover. I encourage you to do the same. If your child is old enough and you have a relationship, I encourage you to listen to their heart and continue to walk in the love that you began in, sacrificial love.

Christ's love was sacrificial. He is our example and you may be surprised to find out you have a lot in common with Him. Read this account of how He loved.

Isaiah 53 (NASB), The Suffering Servant
Who has believed our message?
And to whom has the arm of the LORD been revealed?

"The great thing to remember is that though our feelings come and go God's love for us does not."
—C.S. Lewis

² For He grew up before Him like a tender shoot,
And like a root out of parched ground;
He has no *stately* form or majesty
That we should look upon Him,
Nor appearance that we should be attracted to Him.

³ He was despised and forsaken of men,
A man of sorrows and acquainted with grief;
And like one from whom men hide their face
He was despised, and we did not esteem Him.

⁴ Surely our griefs He Himself bore,
And our sorrows He carried;
Yet we ourselves esteemed Him stricken,
Smitten of God, and afflicted.
⁵ But He was pierced through for our transgressions,
He was crushed for our iniquities;
The chastening for our well-being *fell* upon Him,
And by His scourging we are healed.
⁶ All of us like sheep have gone astray,
Each of us has turned to his own way;
But the LORD has caused the iniquity of us all
To fall on Him.

⁷ He was oppressed and He was afflicted,
Yet He did not open His mouth;
Like a lamb that is led to slaughter,
And like a sheep that is silent before its shearers,
So He did not open His mouth.
⁸ By oppression and judgment He was taken away;
And as for His generation, who considered
That He was cut off out of the land of the living
For the transgression of my people, to whom the stroke *was due*?
⁹ His grave was assigned with wicked men,
Yet He was with a rich man in His death,
Because He had done no violence,
Nor was there any deceit in His mouth.

"The great thing to remember is that though our feelings come and go God's love for us does not."
—C.S. Lewis

¹⁰ But the Lord was pleased
To crush Him, putting *Him* to grief;
If He would render Himself *as* a guilt offering,
He will see *His* offspring,
He will prolong *His* days,
And the good pleasure of the Lord will prosper in His hand.
¹¹ As a result of the anguish of His soul,
He will see *it and* be satisfied;
By His knowledge the Righteous One,
My Servant, will justify the many,
As He will bear their iniquities.

¹² Therefore, I will allot Him a portion with the great,
And He will divide the booty with the strong;
Because He poured out Himself to death,
And was numbered with the transgressors;
Yet He Himself bore the sin of many,
And interceded for the transgressors.

Jesus focused on the Loved. He sacrificed for those He loves. He did it deliberately. He did it when others close to Him couldn't understand, didn't agree, would not follow His choice through with Him to the end. It was painful. It was hard. There was public humiliation. Sound familiar?

How can you identify with the suffering of Christ? Christ died for all of your suffering, all of your grief and pain in every moment of this journey from finding out you were pregnant to right now. That is huge.

How has your love and sacrifice of your child changed you? Do you feel/see/ experience any redemption in your life post-placement? What does it look like? How are you loving your child well right now? What do you anticipate your child needing from you in the future? Is there anything you are afraid to tell your child? What is your child, or your child's parents, saying to you now about his/her needs? How can you continue to honor and love your child as he/she grows and changes? What will be/is the hardest part of your story to tell your child? How can you prepare your heart to share all of you with your beloved child?

"The great thing to remember is that though our feelings come and go God's love for us does not."
—C.S. Lewis

"The great thing to remember is that though our feelings come and go God's love for us does not."
—**C.S. Lewis**

"The great thing to remember is that though our feelings come and go God's love for us does not."

—C.S. Lewis

"The great thing to remember is that though our feelings come and go God's love for us does not."

—C.S. Lewis

"The great thing to remember is that though our feelings come and go God's love for us does not."
—**C.S. Lewis**

"The great thing to remember is that though our feelings come and go God's love for us does not."
—**C.S. Lewis**

"The great thing to remember is that though our feelings come and go God's love for us does not."
—**C.S. Lewis**

"The great thing to remember is that though our feelings come and go God's love for us does not."

—**C.S. Lewis**

"The great thing to remember is that though our feelings come and go God's love for us does not."
—**C.S. Lewis**

"The great thing to remember is that though our feelings come and go God's love for us does not."

—**C.S. Lewis**

"The great thing to remember is that though our feelings come and go God's love for us does not."

—**C.S. Lewis**

"The great thing to remember is that though our feelings come and go God's love for us does not."

—C.S. Lewis

"The great thing to remember is that though our feelings come and go God's love for us does not."

—C.S. Lewis

"The great thing to remember is that though our feelings come and go God's love for us does not."
—C.S. Lewis

"The great thing to remember is that though our feelings come and go God's love for us does not."

—C.S. Lewis

_____

_____

_____

_____

_____

_____

_____

_____

_____

_____

_____

_____

_____

_____

_____

_____

_____

_____

_____

_____

_____

_____

"The great thing to remember is that though our feelings come and go God's love for us does not."

—C.S. Lewis

"Beautiful Things" – Gungor, <u>Beautiful Things</u>

All this pain
I wonder if I'll ever find my way
I wonder if my life could really change at all
All this earth
Could all that is lost ever be found
Could a garden come up from this ground at all

You make beautiful things
You make beautiful things out of the dust
You make beautiful things
You make beautiful things out of us

All around
Hope is springing up from this old ground
Out of chaos life is being found in You

You make beautiful things
You make beautiful things out of the dust
You make beautiful things
You make beautiful things out of us

You make beautiful things
You make beautiful things out of the dust
You make beautiful things
You make beautiful things out of us

You make me new, You are making me new
You make me new, You are making me new

You make beautiful things
You make beautiful things out of the dust
You make beautiful things
You make beautiful things out of us

"The great thing to remember is that though our feelings come and go God's love for us does not."
—C.S. Lewis

7

WORTHY TO BE KNOWN

Have you ever played a game where you are blind-folded and you have to stick your hand in different jars with different things to feel? Like peeled grapes that "feel gross" but are in reality good (to most people!), or dry/uncooked beans/rice/etc. that feel good but are in reality gross to eat (when they are dry/uncooked). This game helped me realize something important.

Feelings are not facts; Feelings are guides.

When we feel left out or lesser, those are not facts. The truest thing about you is what God thinks, and friends, God thought, and still thinks, you (yes, you, right now as you are) are worth the life of His Son, Jesus.

What do you think? Do you agree? Do you hold a standard higher than God's? Do you feel unworthy of the life of Christ? The key is not to look at yourself, but at Christ. What does God say about you? Indulge me for a moment.

If any man is in Christ, he is a new creation, the salt of the earth, the light of the world, a child of God, chosen, dearly loved, an heir of God, a citizen of heaven, hidden in Christ with God, righteous, holy, and on and on and on...

Now that you know, do you believe it? And if you believe it, you can live out of the truth of who you are in Him. It's just that simple and just that hard. This is something that you will return to over-and-over throughout your life. So, get comfortable needing to be reminded of who you truly are.

"The great thing to remember is that though our feelings come and go God's love for us does not."
—C.S. Lewis

"Who in the world am I? Ah, that's the great puzzle."
— Lewis Carroll, *Alice in Wonderland*

"Uncensored emotions spell big trouble. Yet, emotions are our most direct reaction to our perception of ourselves and the world around us. Whether positive or negative, feelings put us in touch with our true selves. They are neither good nor bad: They are simply the truth of what's going on in us. **What we do with our feelings will determine whether we live lives of honesty or of deceit.** When submitted to the discretion of a faith-formed intellect, our emotions serve as trustworthy beacons for appropriate action or inaction. The denial, displacement, and repression of feeling thwarts self-intimacy."

— Brennan Manning, *Abba's Child*

What are your feelings toward yourself, your child, your child's parents, your adoption process? How are those feelings guiding you? Are any of those feeling false, or do any of them need to change? What are your feelings about God? Do you think you are worthy to be known? Who have you let in on an intimate level to know you? Who have you revealed your heart to? Can you reveal your heart to God? Do you need to give yourself a clean slate and let God define you? What would you like your clean slate to say about you? What do you like about yourself right now?

Colossians 3:2-4 (NASB)
Set your mind on the things above, not on the things that are on earth. For you have died and your life is hidden with Christ in God. When Christ, who is our life, is revealed, then you also will be revealed with Him in glory.

John 8:31-32 (NASB)
So Jesus was saying to those Jews who had believed Him, "If you continue in My word, *then* you are truly disciples of Mine; and you will know the truth, and the truth will make you free.

"The great thing to remember is that though our feelings come and go God's love for us does not."
—C.S. Lewis

"The great thing to remember is that though our feelings come and go God's love for us does not."
—**C.S. Lewis**

"The great thing to remember is that though our feelings come and go God's love for us does not."
—C.S. Lewis

"The great thing to remember is that though our feelings come and go God's love for us does not."

—C.S. Lewis

"The great thing to remember is that though our feelings come and go God's love for us does not."

—C.S. Lewis

"The great thing to remember is that though our feelings come and go God's love for us does not."
—**C.S. Lewis**

"The great thing to remember is that though our feelings come and go God's love for us does not."

—C.S. Lewis

"The great thing to remember is that though our feelings come and go God's love for us does not."
—**C.S. Lewis**

"The great thing to remember is that though our feelings come and go God's love for us does not."

—C.S. Lewis

_____

_____

_____

_____

_____

_____

_____

_____

_____

_____

_____

_____

_____

_____

_____

_____

_____

_____

_____

_____

_____

"The great thing to remember is that though our feelings come and go God's love for us does not."
—**C.S. Lewis**

"The great thing to remember is that though our feelings come and go God's love for us does not."

—C.S. Lewis

"The great thing to remember is that though our feelings come and go God's love for us does not."

—C.S. Lewis

"The great thing to remember is that though our feelings come and go God's love for us does not."
—**C.S. Lewis**

"The great thing to remember is that though our feelings come and go God's love for us does not."

—**C.S. Lewis**

"The great thing to remember is that though our feelings come and go God's love for us does not."

—C.S. Lewis

"The great thing to remember is that though our feelings come and go God's love for us does not."

—**C.S. Lewis**

"How long is forever?" asked Alice.
"Sometimes, just one second," replied White Rabbit.

— Lewis Carroll, *Alice in Wonderland*

"Dry Bones" – Gungor, <u>Beautiful Things</u>

my soul cries out
my soul cries out for you

these bones cry out
these dry bones cry for you
to live and move
only You
can raise the dead
lift my head up

Jesus, You're the one who saves us
Constantly creates us into something new
Jesus You're the one who finds us
Surely our Messiah will make all things new

"The great thing to remember is that though our feelings come and go God's love for us does not."

—C.S. Lewis

8

LETTING GO

Continually letting go, as this happens in stages, is hard. We think on the front end that we have our adoption plan figured out, and then we find ourselves on our heels post-placement. It's a rude awakening when your sadness follows you out of the hospital. I expected mine to go away eventually, but it didn't. There were aching, empty arms, the longing for my flesh and blood, and the raw craving that swelled up in me. They got further apart in time, but they were still potent when it would come up.

I felt like there was something wrong with me. Some people in my life expected me to be 'over it' by now. This is not something you get over; it is something you move through.

Let me offer you some freedom. It is okay to continue to grieve. It is okay to not have it figured out. If someone tells you that your feelings are wrong, or that you need to stay quiet about it, they are not your friend. Wherever you are, be all there.

"Part of every misery is, so to speak, the misery's shadow or reflection: the fact that you don't merely suffer but have to keep on thinking about the fact that you suffer. I not only live each endless day in grief, but live each day thinking about living each day in grief."

— C.S. Lewis, *A Grief Observed*

Grief pops up at life events, birthdays, holidays, etc. Expect it. My friend Eric told me a story about hiding his hurt in his pocket. You can do this. It may help you to have a stone or an item that you can carry with you. Something that is small, but important. When grief hits, you take your hurt out of your pocket, acknowledge it, hold it, and when you're ready, put it back in your pocket.

"The great thing to remember is that though our feelings come and go God's love for us does not."
—C.S. Lewis

I like this idea because sometimes grief gets so out of control that you can't stop grieving. An item in your pocket *may* help you to grieve in spurts. Especially if you have children at home or are working or going to school, being able to recognize your hurt in a tangible way can prove to be helpful for functioning in your daily life.

Psalms 119:41-50 (NASB)
Remember the word to Your servant,
In which You have made me hope.
This is my comfort in my affliction,
That Your word has revived me.

It's just not simple, is it? You want to hold onto what was and what is, but you have to let go of what is not and what will never be. This pregnancy was beautiful but not ideal. This child is yours but not in your home. You are a mother but you don't mother daily. It's confusing and stretching and painful. I feel you, friend. I so feel that for you and with you.

I wonder if you will consider that your center, your gravity, could be the person of Christ. He holds it all together for me. It's like the roller coaster thing and the flux of emotions. I feel a million different things at once sometimes and I get to unload on God. God is big. He can handle it. So, when I go to Him over and over again and fill another bucket of tears at His feet or bloody my knuckles fighting with Him, I am going to the same place, the same Person. I return to the truest part of me and that pulls all my contrasting parts together. He is the consistent thing in my life. He is not on my roller coaster, but He is with me on the Birthmother Train. I need the comfort of Him, the assurance that I will always find Him in a receptive mood and loving me no matter what I'm doing or feeling. He gives me peace in my chaos.

What have you let go of already? What are you still holding onto? How do you feel when you encounter something or someone that you lost in choosing to place your child for adoption? How do you prepare for the moments of grief? What are some of your triggers? How have you coped in the past? Will an item in your pocket help you? Will joining a support group help you? How can you continue to let go of what is not and stay connected to what is? What is consistent in your life? Who or what gives you peace in your chaos?

These questions may be some that you revisit more than once. Consider leaving room for your heart to change and for more processing as life continues.

"The great thing to remember is that though our feelings come and go God's love for us does not."
—C.S. Lewis

"The great thing to remember is that though our feelings come and go God's love for us does not."
—**C.S. Lewis**

"The great thing to remember is that though our feelings come and go God's love for us does not."
—**C.S. Lewis**

_____

_____

_____

_____

_____

_____

_____

_____

_____

_____

_____

_____

_____

_____

_____

_____

_____

_____

_____

_____

_____

_____

_____

_____

"The great thing to remember is that though our feelings come and go God's love for us does not."

—C.S. Lewis

"The great thing to remember is that though our feelings come and go God's love for us does not."
—**C.S. Lewis**

"The great thing to remember is that though our feelings come and go God's love for us does not."

—C.S. Lewis

"The great thing to remember is that though our feelings come and go God's love for us does not."
—**C.S. Lewis**

"The great thing to remember is that though our feelings come and go God's love for us does not."
—**C.S. Lewis**

"The great thing to remember is that though our feelings come and go God's love for us does not."

—C.S. Lewis

"The great thing to remember is that though our feelings come and go God's love for us does not."

—C.S. Lewis

"The great thing to remember is that though our feelings come and go God's love for us does not."

—**C.S. Lewis**

"The great thing to remember is that though our feelings come and go God's love for us does not."

—C.S. Lewis

"The great thing to remember is that though our feelings come and go God's love for us does not."

—C.S. Lewis

"The great thing to remember is that though our feelings come and go God's love for us does not."

—C.S. Lewis

"The great thing to remember is that though our feelings come and go God's love for us does not."

—C.S. Lewis

"The great thing to remember is that though our feelings come and go God's love for us does not."
—C.S. Lewis

Zephaniah 3:17 (VOICE)

The Eternal your God is standing right here among you,
and He is the champion who will rescue you.
He will joyfully celebrate over you;
He will rest in His love for you;
He will joyfully sing because of you like a new husband.

"The great thing to remember is that though our feelings come and go God's love for us does not."
—C.S. Lewis

9

BIRTHDAYS

Google M.C. Escher's woodcut *Sky and Water 1*.

Looking at this print you may see birds first or fish first, but they are both there. I love Escher's woodcut because the positive and negative spaces exchange over the piece. Both are vital to the piece. During the process of carving the wood, Escher had to make deliberate decisions about where he would make his mark and what he would whittle away. If he hadn't cut the wood, he wouldn't have the story that the drawing tells.

I think this is true for birthmothers. Both the positive and negative 'spaces' or experiences or moments in a birthmother's story are important. They make up the whole of the experience. You can't take the good or bad away, nor can you leave birthmother uncut, and have the same story. And it can change. Things that I thought were negative, like being a birthmother, have changed into positive for me, because I can relate to you and love on you without shame or judgement. You are my people, and I love you. So there!

Our greatest example is Christ. You can't take the suffering away and only have the redemption. Both are important. Both are relevant. We need both the Cross and the Resurrection.

What are the positive parts of your story? What are the negative parts of your story? How have both played a part of your adoption process? Have you tried to hide the negative parts of your story? How can you honor your whole story in your life now, relationship with your child, other relationships?

"The great thing to remember is that though our feelings come and go God's love for us does not."

—C.S. Lewis

Birthdays often bring up both positive and negative feelings. You will remember the moments of joy and feel the gap between being a birthmother and a mother. You do not get to share all of your child's moments on their birthday. It's a loss of life in the midst of the celebration of life every year.

But your child is worthy to be celebrated, even if you are not with them. You can begin traditions of eating cake or writing a letter. My family and I each have a sweet treat (usually a cupcake or cookie) with a candle. We all say a silent prayer or hope for my son and then we sing him Happy Birthday and blow out 'his' candles.

Over time, this very hard day for me every calendar year, March 10th, has become one where I get to share one of God's greatest gifts to me. I get to celebrate him and I get to teach my kids that God makes beauty from ashes and that suffering leads to hope.

What birthday traditions do you honor for your child? If you don't have a tradition for your child's birthday, what would you like to create to commemorate this special day? How can/do you celebrate your child's life throughout the year?

"The great thing to remember is that though our feelings come and go God's love for us does not."
—**C.S. Lewis**

"The great thing to remember is that though our feelings come and go God's love for us does not."
—C.S. Lewis

"The great thing to remember is that though our feelings come and go God's love for us does not."
—C.S. Lewis

"The great thing to remember is that though our feelings come and go God's love for us does not."
—**C.S. Lewis**

"The great thing to remember is that though our feelings come and go God's love for us does not."

—C.S. Lewis

_____

_____

_____

_____

_____

_____

_____

_____

_____

_____

_____

_____

_____

_____

_____

_____

_____

_____

_____

_____

_____

"The great thing to remember is that though our feelings come and go God's love for us does not."

—C.S. Lewis

"The great thing to remember is that though our feelings come and go God's love for us does not."

—C.S. Lewis

"The great thing to remember is that though our feelings come and go God's love for us does not."
—**C.S. Lewis**

"The great thing to remember is that though our feelings come and go God's love for us does not."

—C.S. Lewis

"The great thing to remember is that though our feelings come and go God's love for us does not."
—**C.S. Lewis**

"The great thing to remember is that though our feelings come and go God's love for us does not."
—**C.S. Lewis**

_____

_____

_____

_____

_____

_____

_____

_____

_____

_____

_____

_____

_____

_____

_____

_____

_____

_____

_____

_____

_____

_____

"The great thing to remember is that though our feelings come and go God's love for us does not."

—C.S. Lewis

"The great thing to remember is that though our feelings come and go God's love for us does not."
—**C.S. Lewis**

"The great thing to remember is that though our feelings come and go God's love for us does not."

—C.S. Lewis

"The great thing to remember is that though our feelings come and go God's love for us does not."

—C.S. Lewis

"The great thing to remember is that though our feelings come and go God's love for us does not."
—C.S. Lewis

"If we have no peace, it is because we have forgotten that we belong to each other."

— Mother Teresa

"The great thing to remember is that though our feelings come and go God's love for us does not."

—C.S. Lewis

10

HOLIDAYS (A SPECIAL WORD ABOUT MOTHER'S DAY)

You, friend, are worthy to be known. God says it. I say it. Your child wants to know you.

I have talked to many adult adoptees over the years and they most often want to know their birthmother at some point in their lives. A good way to let them in that is unrelated to the heaviness of adoption is to share your life with them. Sharing Holiday traditions and memories is a great way to give them a piece of who you are and where they come from.

A word about Mother's Day: sucks. Well, that's it…

Seriously, Mother's Day is a huge trigger for grief to pop up. It can be going to church and not being able to stand when they ask all the mothers to stand, because what they mean is women who have or are parenting children. (I hope that's not happening at your church, by the way.) It could be that you are not recognized as a mother by anyone, which is so hurtful. It could be that you are parenting other children, they give you a flower and celebrate you, and yet, it still doesn't feel complete somehow. Maybe it's just a nationally honored day of shame for you. Whatever it is, Mother's Day can be, will likely be, a hard day every year.

My best advice, for whatever it's worth, prepare for it. Make it a 'treat-yo-self' day! Go to eat at your favorite spot. Curl up with a good book. Watch your favorite movie. Surround yourself with people who support you and love you and give you the freedom to be where your at and feel how you feel. And give yourself the freedom to have fluctuating emotions. Don't get stuck. Push through the moments, know that it's one day, and you're not alone. Connect with your support group or an online forum for birthmothers if you don't have anyone present in your life to reach out to.

"The great thing to remember is that though our feelings come and go God's love for us does not."
—C.S. Lewis

Your role as a mother cannot be justified by anyone. They will not do it justice. Don't rely on them.

Take courage, friend! You are a mother. You made an enormously selfless parenting decision. Know that you are loved and accepted by God, and treat yourself accordingly.

What is your favorite thing about the Holidays? What is your best Holiday memory? Does your family have certain traditions on certain holidays? Do you go to a particular place for Thanksgiving or have special people over for dinner? Are there sports traditions you keep? Food traditions? Religious traditions?

How can you prepare right now for Mother's Day? What do you anticipate will be your biggest challenge? What are some ways you can celebrate yourself and the choice of life?

Flesh out your memories and thoughts here. Consider writing something you would like to be a tradition between you and your child. Then, go get some paper/cards and write. Write personal notes to your child about what you love about the Holidays.

"The great thing to remember is that though our feelings come and go God's love for us does not."

—C.S. Lewis

"The great thing to remember is that though our feelings come and go God's love for us does not."
—**C.S. Lewis**

_____

_____

_____

_____

_____

_____

_____

_____

_____

_____

_____

_____

_____

_____

_____

_____

_____

_____

_____

_____

_____

_____

"The great thing to remember is that though our feelings come and go God's love for us does not."

—**C.S. Lewis**

_____

_____

_____

_____

_____

_____

_____

_____

_____

_____

_____

_____

_____

_____

_____

_____

_____

_____

_____

_____

_____

_____

"The great thing to remember is that though our feelings come and go God's love for us does not."

—C.S. Lewis

"The great thing to remember is that though our feelings come and go God's love for us does not."

—C.S. Lewis

"The great thing to remember is that though our feelings come and go God's love for us does not."

—C.S. Lewis

"The great thing to remember is that though our feelings come and go God's love for us does not."
—**C.S. Lewis**

"The great thing to remember is that though our feelings come and go God's love for us does not."
—C.S. Lewis

"The great thing to remember is that though our feelings come and go God's love for us does not."

—C.S. Lewis

"The great thing to remember is that though our feelings come and go God's love for us does not."

—C.S. Lewis

"The great thing to remember is that though our feelings come and go God's love for us does not."

—C.S. Lewis

"The great thing to remember is that though our feelings come and go God's love for us does not."
—C.S. Lewis

"The great thing to remember is that though our feelings come and go God's love for us does not."

—C.S. Lewis

"O Holy Night"

**Long lay the world
in sin and error pining
'til He appeared
and the soul felt its worth**

"The great thing to remember is that though our feelings come and go God's love for us does not."
—**C.S. Lewis**

11

CHRISTMAS

I challenge you to go through Christmas and not think about gifts. You can't do it, can you? Gifts are part of this time. Gifts are part of our lives. God gave us the ultimate gift in His Son Jesus. We celebrate the gift of Him, of His life, on Christmas. That is a great thing!

Psalm 127:3 (NASB)
Behold, children are a gift of the LORD,
The fruit of the womb is a reward.

We also can celebrate the gifts we have been given. Sometimes Christmas can be a hard time for birthmothers. We feel the loss, we notice the hole. But friend, I encourage you this season to look on what you do have, to celebrate the life that you helped create. This child is a gift.

The Word says that children are a blessing from the Lord. It doesn't say the children you parent, or the ones who are born to married people. It says children, all children, your child. Your child is a gift from the Lord. That is amazing! And if your child is a gift, how can you share your gift with the world, the way God did?

This doesn't have to be talking about your child or your choice. Sharing this gift can be as simple as volunteering at a crisis pregnancy center or feeding the poor. Maybe you are called to give a love offering to your church or a ministry you are passionate about? Do something in the name of Jesus because of the gift of your child. Share His love this Season.

"The great thing to remember is that though our feelings come and go God's love for us does not."
—**C.S. Lewis**

"The great thing to remember is that though our feelings come and go God's love for us does not."
—**C.S. Lewis**

"The great thing to remember is that though our feelings come and go God's love for us does not."

—C.S. Lewis

"The great thing to remember is that though our feelings come and go God's love for us does not."

—**C.S. Lewis**

_____

_____

_____

_____

_____

_____

_____

_____

_____

_____

_____

_____

_____

_____

_____

_____

_____

_____

_____

_____

_____

_____

"The great thing to remember is that though our feelings come and go God's love for us does not."
—**C.S. Lewis**

"The great thing to remember is that though our feelings come and go God's love for us does not."

—**C.S. Lewis**

"The great thing to remember is that though our feelings come and go God's love for us does not."
—**C.S. Lewis**

"The great thing to remember is that though our feelings come and go God's love for us does not."
—**C.S. Lewis**

"The great thing to remember is that though our feelings come and go God's love for us does not."

—C.S. Lewis

"The great thing to remember is that though our feelings come and go God's love for us does not."
—C.S. Lewis

"The great thing to remember is that though our feelings come and go God's love for us does not."

—C.S. Lewis

"The great thing to remember is that though our feelings come and go God's love for us does not."
—C.S. Lewis

"The great thing to remember is that though our feelings come and go God's love for us does not."
—**C.S. Lewis**

"The great thing to remember is that though our feelings come and go God's love for us does not."
—C.S. Lewis

"The great thing to remember is that though our feelings come and go God's love for us does not."
—C.S. Lewis

"Courage is what it takes to stand up and speak; courage is also what it takes to sit down and listen."

— Winston Churchill

"The way to fight shame and to honor who we are is by sharing our experience with someone who has earned the right to hear it."

— Brené Brown

"The great thing to remember is that though our feelings come and go God's love for us does not."

—C.S. Lewis

12

YOUR STORY

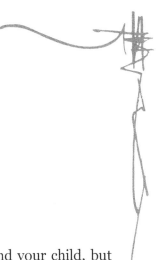

Your story is important—period. It is not only important to you and your child, but to the world and to me as well. Your story lets me know I'm not alone. Your story tells about pain and joy cast in leading roles of your life. I get that.

I believe that telling your story is important because that is what God does. He tells His story over and over to people, through people.

You will find that sharing your story, coming out of hiding, has power. It empowers you, it connects you, and it strengthens you. Not everyone will get it. Let me assure you of that, but let me also say that just because some people can't handle your information, doesn't mean it should never be told. You can and should choose your audience. If you need to be accepted in that moment, don't tell the ignorant. Call a friend who has been there. If it is more important to get it out, than tell it.

Also, there is something to be said for the integrity and freedom of living your story. When you hide your story, you hide part of yourself. Hiding reeks of fear. Fear is not good for you—plain and simple.

My encouragement is two-fold. Start with a simple truth: Jesus can relate to you, and you can relate to Him. He loved and rejoiced and He grieved and sacrificed. You can relate to those things. He is relational. Jesus died to have a relationship with you.

This makes your relationship with Him more tangible. How did I figure this out? I looked at the truth, the eternal, and realized our stories, our temporary, should not be the defining characteristics of God. But God, who He was, is, and will be, should be *our* defining characteristic.

"The great thing to remember is that though our feelings come and go God's love for us does not."
—C.S. Lewis

I challenge you to let Jesus define who He is to you, so you can think rightly about God. My hope is that you will begin to think about God in a way that is true and that changes you.

"What comes into your mind when you think about God is the most important thing about you."

— A.W. Tozer, *Knowledge of the Holy*

Just stop for a minute and be there. Think about God. What comes into your mind? Is it consistent with who God says He is? I wonder how your story would change if your thoughts about God changed. I wonder if you have misinterpreted Him through other people, as we all have, what you may have misunderstood or been taught wrong about Him.

I truly believe that your story is folded into a bigger story that God is telling. I truly believe that you loved like God when you placed your child, even if you didn't love like Him consciously. God placed His child too. With Joseph and Mary, God entrusted them to raise Jesus on this earth. God never stopped loving Jesus.

Wow! Your story is so similar. God is not so different from you, and you are not so different from Him. You have a lot in common, and you should because you are made in His image.

My point is this: If you begin to think rightly about God, you will begin to think rightly about yourself. Your story is worth being told and hearing over and over again because your story is God's story. It is one of love and redemption, loss and pain. It's not pretty, but it is beautiful.

When you think of God, how do you feel about Him? How do you think He feels about you? How do you feel when you think about God? Do you ever wish God would have written a different story for you? Are you angry with God about any part of your story? Does God ever surprise you? Do you believe God enjoys you? Do you believe God likes who you are? Do you believe God loves you?

"The great thing to remember is that though our feelings come and go God's love for us does not."

—C.S. Lewis

"The great thing to remember is that though our feelings come and go God's love for us does not."
—C.S. Lewis

"The great thing to remember is that though our feelings come and go God's love for us does not."
—**C.S. Lewis**

_____

_____

_____

_____

_____

_____

_____

_____

_____

_____

_____

_____

_____

_____

_____

_____

_____

_____

_____

_____

"The great thing to remember is that though our feelings come and go God's love for us does not."

—C.S. Lewis

"The great thing to remember is that though our feelings come and go God's love for us does not."
—**C.S. Lewis**

"The great thing to remember is that though our feelings come and go God's love for us does not."
—**C.S. Lewis**

"The great thing to remember is that though our feelings come and go God's love for us does not."

—C.S. Lewis

"The great thing to remember is that though our feelings come and go God's love for us does not."
—C.S. Lewis

"The great thing to remember is that though our feelings come and go God's love for us does not."

—C.S. Lewis

_____

_____

_____

_____

_____

_____

_____

_____

_____

_____

_____

_____

_____

_____

_____

_____

_____

_____

_____

_____

_____

_____

"The great thing to remember is that though our feelings come and go God's love for us does not."

—C.S. Lewis

"The great thing to remember is that though our feelings come and go God's love for us does not."
—C.S. Lewis

"The great thing to remember is that though our feelings come and go God's love for us does not."
—C.S. Lewis

"The great thing to remember is that though our feelings come and go God's love for us does not."

—**C.S. Lewis**

"The great thing to remember is that though our feelings come and go God's love for us does not."

—C.S. Lewis

"The great thing to remember is that though our feelings come and go God's love for us does not."

—C.S. Lewis

_____

_____

_____

_____

_____

_____

_____

_____

_____

_____

_____

_____

_____

_____

_____

_____

_____

_____

_____

"The great thing to remember is that though our feelings come and go God's love for us does not."

—C.S. Lewis

"God cannot give us a happiness and peace apart from Himself, because it is not there. There is no such thing."

— C. S. Lewis

Love will surely break your heart
Then set you free
"Love in High Places" – Kimbra, <u>The Golden Echo</u>

"The great thing to remember is that though our feelings come and go God's love for us does not."

—**C.S. Lewis**

13

MOVING FROM GRIEF TO CELEBRATION

Romans 5:1-5 (VOICE)
5 Since we have been *acquitted and* made right through faith, we are able to experience *true and lasting* peace with God through our Lord Jesus, the Anointed One, *the Liberating King*. ² Jesus leads us into a place of *radical* grace where we are able to celebrate the hope of experiencing God's glory. ³ And that's not all. We also celebrate in seasons of suffering because we know that when we suffer we develop endurance, ⁴ which shapes our characters. When our characters are refined, we learn what it means to hope *and anticipate God's goodness*. ⁵ And hope will never fail to satisfy our deepest need because the Holy Spirit that was given to us has flooded our hearts with God's love.

See the progression, or exchange if you will, from suffering to hope. Hope, which comes from suffering, will never fail to satisfy our deepest need. Friends, this changes everything. This is how I move from the grief to the celebration of adoption. My deepest needs are met in God's goodness and His love. We hurt in pain and we heal in pain. This suffering is both/and. This hurts and this heals.

"God enters through the wound."

— C.G. Jung

"The great thing to remember is that though our feelings come and go God's love for us does not."
—C.S. Lewis

This wound heals me. Being a birthmother is carrying a wound. We might not call it that, but we relate to that language. So, the idea that God enters through the wound gives the wound purpose, holy purpose. Having abundant life includes the wound. Doesn't Jesus model this for us? Don't we wear crosses around our neck, the wound that healed?

This is the part where you see that your need is not met in your child, but in God. Sometimes I think we birthmothers confuse our loss with our need to be loved. We place the burden of filling a hole in our hearts on a child given to us and given by us. We may even think that if we had them back it would make all the difference. My friends, I don't want you to believe this lie. I don't want you stuck in your grief. I don't want you to idolize your child. Jesus, God, the hope found in Him—that is Who is meant to fill the hole in your heart.

The loss of your child through adoption is not the only loss you have. There are many others. The loss of the ideal pregnancy. The loss of parenting. The loss of perception (i.e. you're not who or where you thought you were). Maybe the loss of relationships. The loss of identity as your child's only mother. The list can go on and on.

So, when suffering comes, go to the Lord with the wound in your chest. Let Him clean it, fill it and heal it. What does that look like? It can be as simple as this.

deep breath "God, it hurts."

That one moment of vulnerability takes you to your Source and it reveals you. The rest is up to Him.

Getting real is better than getting better. I pray you are real every season of suffering, so you can know real hope.

What does getting real mean to you? What does getting real look like? What do you need to say in your suffering that you haven't ever said? What do you need to reveal to God about your heart, feelings, and/or circumstances?

Do you believe you can be healed through a wound? Has your choice to place your child healed you in any way or area of your life so far? How would you like for your placement to look in five/ten years? What other losses have you suffered? How do those losses play into your grief over placing your child?

"The great thing to remember is that though our feelings come and go God's love for us does not."
—C.S. Lewis

"The great thing to remember is that though our feelings come and go God's love for us does not."
—**C.S. Lewis**

"The great thing to remember is that though our feelings come and go God's love for us does not."
—C.S. Lewis

"The great thing to remember is that though our feelings come and go God's love for us does not."
—C.S. Lewis

"The great thing to remember is that though our feelings come and go God's love for us does not."
—**C.S. Lewis**

"The great thing to remember is that though our feelings come and go God's love for us does not."
—**C.S. Lewis**

"The great thing to remember is that though our feelings come and go God's love for us does not."

—C.S. Lewis

"The great thing to remember is that though our feelings come and go God's love for us does not."

—C.S. Lewis

"The great thing to remember is that though our feelings come and go God's love for us does not."
—**C.S. Lewis**

"The great thing to remember is that though our feelings come and go God's love for us does not."

—C.S. Lewis

"The great thing to remember is that though our feelings come and go God's love for us does not."

—C.S. Lewis

"The great thing to remember is that though our feelings come and go God's love for us does not."

—**C.S. Lewis**

"The great thing to remember is that though our feelings come and go God's love for us does not."

—C.S. Lewis

"The great thing to remember is that though our feelings come and go God's love for us does not."

—C.S. Lewis

"The great thing to remember is that though our feelings come and go God's love for us does not."

—C.S. Lewis

"The great thing to remember is that though our feelings come and go God's love for us does not."
—**C.S. Lewis**

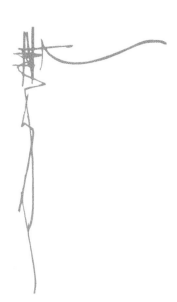

"I'm here. I love you. I don't care if you need to stay up crying all night long, I will stay with you. If you need the medication again, go ahead and take it—I will love you through that, as well. If you don't need the medication, I will love you, too. There's nothing you can ever do to lose my love. I will protect you until you die, and after your death I will still protect you. I am stronger than Depression and I am braver than Loneliness and nothing will ever exhaust me."

— Elizabeth Gilbert, Eat, Pray, Love

"The great thing to remember is that though our feelings come and go God's love for us does not."

—C.S. Lewis

14

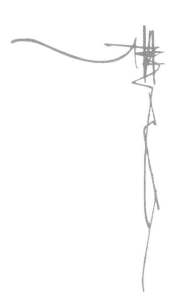

20 QUESTIONS

One of the harder parts about sharing your story with people who don't understand is that the questions get weird, rude, and/or invasive. The comments can also be over the top. It's frustrating.

Be prepared for them. Know they will come. Ask any birthmother. They will come, and sometimes they are from the sweetest people, who mean well. One piece of advice: allow others to be ignorant. Like I said at the beginning, you don't know what you don't know, and friend, they don't know. Educate them. The best way to combat ignorance is education.

So, here are several of the questions/comments I hear most. Indulge me while I list a few and give a brief, or not so brief, retort.

Birthmothers are my heroes.

Really? I'm flattered. I don't feel like a heroine for continuing on in the deep mud of self-exposure, I feel more like an old paint rag that dried in a certain position and now I can't get out.

(I must reference my very wise director Becky, who says, "You may not feel like a hero, but your choice of life was heroic." After working in adoption and trying to talk girls out of abortion. I have to agree.)

"The great thing to remember is that though our feelings come and go God's love for us does not."
—C.S. Lewis

It's funny to hear that though now that I am raising two children, I am intensely aware that adoptive parents are my heroes. They step right into the middle of their child's story and go. They care for these children in a physical way on a daily basis that I could not even imagine when I placed my son. They tend to their children's hearts and hold them close.

Here are a couple of blog posts of mine that I hope help enlighten you on the subject of my heroics.

Balancing the Scales

For a long time I talked about my adoption process like this, "I sinned, and then I fixed it by doing the right thing."

That kind of talk turns my stomach now.

As if I could do the right thing and the wrong was then dismissed. There is a young man who might say otherwise. I know I do.

Why do I still grieve this much if the wrong was made right?
I have felt the need to show people I am better than I was when I did *that one sin*. I think people like to hear that sometimes. It makes them feel more comfortable. It makes me more acceptable.

Am I?

I think when I focus on *that one sin* and call it out like a snake-charming preacher, I reinforce this idea in my mind. I was bad. I am better now. And I need to be. I need to be better or what in the world did I do that for? If I'm not better than what does that say about God?

I'm so responsible for Him, right? There have been times when I have felt that way. A lot of times. It's exhausting. I'm exhausted.

Why do we preach 'CHOOSE LIFE' and then, make women facing unplanned pregnancy pay for their choice of life? I read a quote last week that said, "I would rather take my abortion to God, than my unplanned pregnancy to my church."

"The great thing to remember is that though our feelings come and go God's love for us does not."
—C.S. Lewis

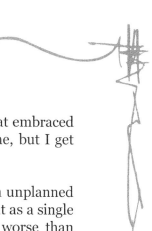

Friends, I get that. That was me, and this is grievous.

Not every church is like that. I was a part of a church in Charlotte that embraced me, my story and my process. So, it's not a blanket statement by me, but I get where she is coming from.

I feel like the Church has suggested adoption as the end all, be all in unplanned pregnancy, and I wonder why? Why is it better to place than to parent as a single person? Is it because single parents struggle? Does that make it worse than adoption? Do you think birthparents don't struggle? Is God not in the struggle? And if so, then how do we determine which woman should struggle one way and which should struggle another?
Maybe I'm just tired of trying to justify my actions. Maybe I'm just tired of trying to make up for something that I did when I was so young, so lost.

Here's the thing: **I don't justify myself**, and therein lies the problem. I never can justify myself, and I never will. I have been trying to balance a scale that I was never meant to be on.

I have been applauded for supposedly doing so. People celebrate my actions, like I did something redemptive. *I wonder if my son thinks so?*

I hate the words, "You did the right thing," or " the best thing."

Did I?

I'm not saying I doubt my decision. I don't. I'm just saying when it comes to unplanned pregnancy, let's stop pretending like we have the answer and that one answer is adoption. Let's stop selling it like, "There are so many infertile couples out there." I doubt these sweet couples want their infertility flashed like a car commercial.

It's hard for me because I can't disconnect the sacrifice from the selfishness. It's two sides of the same tree, good and evil. I need something different than this. I need something other.

The truth of my redemption being only in Christ relieves me, though I admit it is still a challenge to articulate that inside of my adoption process. I know other birthmoms who feel the same way. If these birthmoms are not rooted in the

"The great thing to remember is that though our feelings come and go God's love for us does not."
—C.S. Lewis

goodness of God, if they don't know the saving power of the Cross and the newness of Life found in Christ, they may feel like I did for years, responsible for making up for *that one sin.*

Here is my encouragement to you, friends, and to you, Church. When you encounter a birthmother/first mother/biological mother brave enough to expose herself to you, please, don't condemn or commend her for her act of placement. Please, *please,* don't pat her on the back. Take it from me, it is awkward for her at best and it only reinforces the lie that she can somehow do enough good to abolish *that one sin.* Instead, offer her enough love and freedom to talk about it how she wants to, feel how she is feeling, and be where she is at in the process.

Take Jesus' example in John 8. "Neither do I condemn you."

He didn't clothe that woman, and you don't have to either. He didn't clothe her because that is not what she needed. He gave her acceptance, forgiveness, and grace. And it wasn't because He had to; He gave those things because that is who He is. There is no such thing as reluctant grace, that's simply masked pride. If you are in Christ, you can walk in acceptance, forgiveness and grace.

You can because He does.

Take courage, friends. Jesus' action on the Cross justifies any woman who is in Him, even if she is facing (or has faced) an unplanned pregnancy. Jesus is enough, and Jesus is who she needs.

Give her Jesus.

And a follow up...

Jesus though...

Just when I'm writing about it being **my turn**...

Over the last three days I have had the privilege of hearing three birthmother's stories. It rocked me to my core.

Let me start at the beginning.

"The great thing to remember is that though our feelings come and go God's love for us does not."
—C.S. Lewis

Thursday night I was in the post-placement support group that I facilitate for birthmothers. It's called Imprint. An imprint is a lasting mark made by pressure. It is something that happens to a whole—meaning, it is not the whole. I think this describes a birthmother perfectly, no matter what her individual adoption experience is/was/will be.

Anyway, I'm sitting there and we are talking about annoying/hard questions and/or comments we encounter. Here were some of them:

Didn't you love your baby?
Aren't you undermining the parents' authority by being in relationship with/seeing the kid you gave up?
Just say you don't have a baby because you don't have a baby.
Can you get him back?
Where is your baby?
Why can't you just move on and forget about it?
You're going to hell.
You will lose all of your blessings and never get blessed again.
How many children do you have?

But there are others. We started with the negative ones, but there are others.

You're my hero.
You did the best thing for him.
You are so courageous.
I'm so proud of you!
You're story is amazing.
He is so lucky.

All of this reminded me of **my post** the other day about not condemning nor clothing a woman caught in adultery. I said to the group, "I feel like half of the people are dragging us through the town and into the Temple naked and the other half are trying to clothe us or politely ignore that we are naked." Everyone in the room could relate to that, each of them experiencing both sides of this story portrayed for us in John 8.

And I feel like there was a time when I stood before Him with disbelief. *What could He possibly offer me that is any different?*

"The great thing to remember is that though our feelings come and go God's love for us does not."
—C.S. Lewis

Jesus though...

He is the One who does not condemn you, nor does He clothe you, but He frees you so that you stand in His presence (and in the Temple), as you are—exposed— with your head lifted to Him. **The nakedness doesn't shame you anymore, it just bears witness to the saving power of Christ, who saves us in ways that we need most.**

I wonder if there were others near that woman. I wonder if any other adulterers understood that day that Jesus loves and forgives and frees them too. I wonder if they revealed themselves to God and found that they are loved, accepted, worthy, and secure in His love.

I want to believe that when we are naked in the Temple and the streets and in prayer and in relationship, when we bear witness to Jesus through our story, others are able to understand Him better, encounter Him and receive freedom. I believe that is the power of story. I think Hebrews 11 agrees with me.

I went home thinking about that. How these women reveal themselves to each other in our group in a real and surprisingly inviting way. All are welcome. None are judged. And in that, the healing, miraculous and minute, happens.

So, here I am talking about being so sad I can barely stand it because of the digression and coming death of my mom...Here I am wondering if Jesus is with me even here in this dark hour, and Friday morning at work we have scheduled a videographer to come and help us tell the "birthmother story" through three different women. Being the Pregnancy Counselor, I am to be with them. They are to tell their story to me.

I sat in three different rooms with three different women, and friends, I *wept*. These stories revealed Jesus—Jesus in hurt, in healing, in joy, in pain, in uncertainty, and in me. These stories were a reflection of the Cross *and* the Resurrection. I drew closer to Him after witnessing these women naked before me and hearing of their encounter with Jesus.

"Yes, even here."

I have big love for you, friends. Big love. And I am praying that you are naked and unashamed to tell your story, to live your story out loud. Whatever that looks like in your life, it is a witness to who God is and how He loves us, all of us, no matter

"The great thing to remember is that though our feelings come and go God's love for us does not."

—C.S. Lewis

where we are physically, emotionally, and/or spiritually.

Even if your story is unresolved, especially if it is unresolved—and all of our physical and emotional stories are unresolved this side of Heaven—I hope you are sharing it. God loves process. He is in it. *Even here.*

Why did you give your baby away?

In March of 2000 I handed my son over to his parents. I literally stood there and gave him to his mother. It was a moment most hated and most cherished by me. It was a time in my life that I relive over and over and still find it hard to come away unscathed. In fact, I spent years of my life grieving it and holding onto it and longing for him. I dumped a pile of money into therapy and antidepressants to be able to function on a daily basis.

And the lurking question is *why*. Why did I place my child for adoption?

To answer that question I would have to begin by talking about love. Love is often mistaken for street kiosk knockoffs like lust or pleasure. In this culture I find we throw the word love around like a little league player throws a baseball in his big debut, often and careless. It is common to hear someone talk about love flippantly. *I love those earrings*, or *I love the way you write*. Perhaps it is about a person. *I love his abs*, or *I love how funny she is*. There is also the occasional, *I love Theo James.*

But is this love? Or are we using a word in a way that it was not meant to be used? What is love truly, and how do we know we are in love?

Love is perhaps best defined by C. S. Lewis. He said, "Love is not merely affectionate feeling, but a steady wish for the loved person's ultimate good as far as it can be obtained." (Interesting how he concentrates on the loved person, not the lover.)

"The great thing to remember is that though our feelings come and go God's love for us does not."
—**C.S. Lewis**

I am fortunate to know this kind of love. If you are a parent you know that you are connected to your children in an unimaginable way that alters you. Being a birthmother does not make that bond less. In fact, it may be heightened to a degree. Sophia Loren said, "When you are a mother, you are never really alone in your thoughts. A mother always has to think twice, once for herself and once for her child." This is why birthmothers place their children for adoption. We are thinking of our children and making an honest effort to love them well.

I was watching *Downton Abbey* recently and a woman who had gotten pregnant out of wedlock chose to keep her son instead of placing him with his rich grandparents. I was not disturbed by her choice until she explained why. She said, "What will [he] need more than his mother's love?" I cringed.

While this may seem noble to some, I find it rather selfish. When loving someone well, shouldn't we always be focused on them? I'm not suggesting being a doormat, for who benefits from that? I am merely saying that love is unselfish, and just so you know, my Baby Dylan (who is a teenager now) **has my love,** my thoughts, my prayers.

Why did I place Baby Dylan for adoption? I wanted him to have a chance at a full life. I wanted his soul to stir when he considered love and know that love is not self-seeking. It bears all things, believes all things, hopes all things, and endures all things. I wanted him to experience a love that did not fail him; a love that is a steady wish for his ultimate good as far as it can be obtained.

Can you get him back?

Oh man! Where do I begin...

No, I can't get him back. There is a legal process in adoption. I relinquished my rights knowing full-well what I was doing and at that time in the state I was in the "legal risk period" or the amount of time I had to revoke my consent was seven days. So, that has passed long ago.

"The great thing to remember is that though our feelings come and go God's love for us does not."
—C.S. Lewis

It's more than the ignorance of the legal system though. This question implies that I made a mistake by placing him. Now, let me just stop and say that there are some birthmothers who think they have made a mistake, and that is different from what I am talking about here. The troublesome thing for me is when someone else thinks I have made a mistake.

Living with this decision is already hard enough without others questioning you. *Can you get him back* leads me to believe you think I screwed up by choosing adoption. It disrespects my parenting decision and undermines my plan that I worked hard to figure out and put into place. It dismisses how I love him and long for him. And quite frankly, it just pisses me off.

Can I get him back? No, but you can go away.

Does my birthmother ever think about me?

Does the sun rise in the east and set in the west? Perhaps this question is too easy for me to answer. Being on this side of the adoption triangle, I see it all so clearly. My answer is a resounding YES! Every birthmother I have ever talked to speaks of how much she thinks of her child. I have never met one that said she never thinks about her child. That being said, that easy flippant answer, let me delve into what I think is more important than whether my birthmother ever thinks about me or not.

When my birthmother thinks about me, *what is she thinking?* The 'what' is the real question, I think. After talking to numerous adoptees and being asked the question, "Does my birthmother ever think about me?" I get a follow up question that begins, inevitably with 'what.'

In my own experience, the things I think about when I think of my son are varied. Is he happy? Does he ever think about me? For every person this will be different, but rest assured, she thinks of you.

"The great thing to remember is that though our feelings come and go God's love for us does not."
—C.S. Lewis

How do you live with no shame?

There are a great number of people, some of my family members included, who think I should not talk about being a birthmother—ever. They believe that being a birthmother is something to be ashamed of. This is incredibly frustrating and hurtful. I do not in any way believe that being a birthmother is shameful. Nor do I think God wants me to be ashamed.

Don't get me wrong. There was shame. If you read my book there is a moment where I become aware of where I went wrong and am ashamed. For me, having sex before I was married when I believe in the institution of marriage the way God intended is the shameful bit. Not the pregnancy. The pregnancy is a by-product of the sin, not the sin itself.

More than that, being responsible with how you handle the consequences to your choices should be considered honorable. Let's not forget that some of the greatest people in the Bible were a hot mess. Don't underestimate the power of God. He redeems every single moment. He makes all things new. He creates beauty from ashes.

I could never do that.

I have heard this confession from countless individuals. Some say it when I tell my story, trying to make me feel like I am more than what I am. Some say it as a negative response, trying to tell me they are more than I am. It can be confusing sometimes what they mean exactly. But I want to offer you a thought. Maybe you are judging your statement on your own experiences.

If you had no money to care for a child growing in your belly, you might consider it. If you were not respected as a parent by your parents now, you might think it over. If you were going to take your child into an unhealthy and/or unsafe environment, that could be a factor in placing your child for adoption. If you had no job, no partner, no means of transportation. If you were stuck in your current grievous situation, if you already had more children than you could take care of. And the list goes on.

"The great thing to remember is that though our feelings come and go God's love for us does not."
—C.S. Lewis

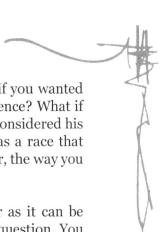

What if you loved your child more than you loved yourself? What if you wanted more for him? What if you thought only of him—his life, his innocence? What if you took into account his Christmases and birthdays? What if you considered his health physically, socially, and emotionally? What if your child was a race that your family would not accept? What if you did not want him to suffer, the way you know he would if he were to stay with you?

If you laid aside everything but your child's ultimate good, as far as it can be obtained, then there would be no maybe or if. There would be no question. You would be compelled by love to love your child well, to love him the whole way. You would surrender any right you thought you had or deserved. You would give up your agenda and you would place all of your love into the single sacrificial act of giving your child a love greater than you. You would give your child a love that keeps on loving. You wouldn't question it. You would do it.

You would do it hurting. Certainly you would feel the loss. But when considering adoption, most birthparents don't focus on their loss, but on their child's gain. What parent, I ask you, what good and loving parent does any different?

You're so brave.

Don't even go there. I don't feel brave. I feel like I screwed up and then did the best I could for this little innocent. I was terrified. I was alone. I was young and ignorant. But I'm educated now, and honey, I'm not brave. I save that stuff for Tris & Four.

You're going to hell.

Actually, I'm saved by the blood of the Lamb. If you don't like that we will 'breathe the same air' in Heaven for all eternity, take it up with God. Oh, and friend, full disclosure: He is the one who invited me.

"The great thing to remember is that though our feelings come and go God's love for us does not."
—C.S. Lewis

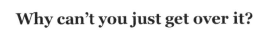

Why can't you just get over it?

Again, I have to offer a blog post of mine to help explain...

Pulled Taut

Today was the day that my daughter started Kindergarten. It was a big day for both of us. I walked her in the pouring rain to her school and down the hall. Tomorrow I will not get to go to her classroom. She is a big girl now. But today, I got to go. Hand-in-hand, we walked and I looked at her. I am so fond of her. She is light and salt and a blessing. She looked back at me and gave a hint of a smile. She was excited!

In these innocent moments, these milestones, I often have company—birthmother grief. It's unforgiving and quick, like the thud of a punch on my cheek. She found her name and sat in her chair. I got down on her level and looked her in the eyes. Then, kneeling there beside my sweet daughter, I lost it.

I kissed her goodbye. I walked out of the classroom and went to my car with tears falling as freely as the rain. I felt a shadow. I felt like an elephant was sitting on my chest. I felt a sense of guilt; this was my daughter's big day. I felt tired. I have been running this race a long time.

Last year I took a job as a Pregnancy Counselor, and this job has put my personal story front and center. I see women everyday walking through different parts of a narrative I have lived. While I am honored to be a small part of their story, it still surprises me how true my Pregnancy Counselor advice is for *myself*.

I have waxed poetically about resurfacing grief. Last month at Imprint, the post-placement support group that I facilitate, I talked about it like it was for the other birthmothers in the room. But God knew it was for me.

"Grief comes up at life events. It doesn't get easier; you begin to recognize it. When it comes up, take a good look at it, hold it, allow yourself to feel it, and give yourself grace."

This morning, I grieved missing the joy of taking Dylan to his first day of school. I felt the distance between us, between parenting and birthparenting.

"The great thing to remember is that though our feelings come and go God's love for us does not."
—C.S. Lewis

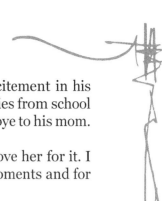

It's not just the milestones I miss, but the moments too. The excitement in his eyes as he learns. The thrill of running on the playground. The stories from school about his day. The little moments, where he smiles and waves goodbye to his mom.

His mom who takes him to school, not me. And I love her and I love her for it. I love her for all of it. For providing for him and for catching the moments and for treasuring him. I am thankful.

Still, on days like today, I can't help but feel the pull in a million different directions, like my heart is a preschool parachute.

Grief comes at life events. It doesn't get easier, you begin to recognize it.

I recognize it.

I know what this is, I think. I take a deep breath. I begin to drive, and I give in to it. I proceed to bawl my eyes out the whole way to work.

And as I park my car, I remember playing with a parachute in Mrs. Diven's P.E. class. I remember the way the parachute works. Pulled from every direction so tight it might split in two, we would hold on and yank that thing in a million directions. Everyone got to play. Everyone was needed to participate and make the parachute work.

It was a group effort.
And I wonder then, about my heart. I feel it being pulled. I feel the danger of it splitting in two. Joy for Cadence. Sadness over Dylan. Pride in my children. Grief over my children. The sweet gains. The significant losses. The hopes, the anticipations, the hurts, and the fears. My heart feels them all.

And I wonder about God. Jesus was a man well-aquatinted with grief and the Savior. He was moved with compassion and had righteous anger in the Temple. He commanded demons and He wept.

And I wonder about that preschool parachute. How it only works with a group of individuals working together all around the edges. How pulling it taut allows it to work properly. How each person attached to the parachute is necessary.

And then I recognize it. This pain reminds me that placing my son for adoption

"The great thing to remember is that though our feelings come and go God's love for us does not."
—C.S. Lewis

was the most loving, hardest thing I have ever done—still, to this day. I welcome the reminder. I take a good look at it, hold it, allow myself to feel it, and give myself grace.

This pain is important. This pain is connected to all the other things that I feel. *This* pain lets me know I still love him *this* much.

Do you have any/how many children do you have?

Women who have miscarried, lost children, aborted children, or placed a child for adoption all have one thing in common. We can all relate to the inner turmoil experienced when asked an innocent question. "How many children do you have?"

That all-encompassing, painful question haunts me anytime I meet people. Do I give them the easy answer, the socially acceptable one, or do I give them the real one? And how do I know in the moment which to choose? And why do I feel so guilty if I lie about it, when in general, people don't handle that information well? And yet, how can I feel equally guilty for telling the truth when I choose to? It's such a simple question, and so harmful for me. It smarts like my surrender just happened. It stings me like I just gave Dylan that last kiss.

It strikes me that the reason this is so difficult a question is not because it reminds me. I don't need something like a simple question to remind me of Dylan. I am reminded of him all the time in a million different ways, and most of the time they are joyful reminders, things that cause me to celebrate his life. So, what's the deal?

I think for me it's that I feel like I lose him all over again, if only in a small way. If I deny that he exists, I verbally give him away again. If I tell people that I have three children but I'm raising two, I am doing the same thing differently. Either way it is a separation from him, and I already feel the gap.

How many children do you have is the hardest question I will ever be asked because it keeps the wound open. But God knew that when He changed my view of Dylan in my womb. He knew that wound would keep my eyes trained on Him, my need for Him constant, and for that, I am thankful. I am thankful for the hardest question because I know that my open wound connects me to the Jesus, the One well-acquainted with grief, and I can trust Him with my pain.

"The great thing to remember is that though our feelings come and go God's love for us does not."
—C.S. Lewis

_____

_____

_____

_____

_____

_____

_____

_____

_____

_____

_____

_____

_____

_____

_____

_____

_____

_____

_____

_____

_____

_____

"The great thing to remember is that though our feelings come and go God's love for us does not."
—**C.S. Lewis**

"The great thing to remember is that though our feelings come and go God's love for us does not."
—**C.S. Lewis**

"The great thing to remember is that though our feelings come and go God's love for us does not."

—C.S. Lewis

"The great thing to remember is that though our feelings come and go God's love for us does not."
—C.S. Lewis

"The great thing to remember is that though our feelings come and go God's love for us does not."
                                                                                    —C.S. Lewis

"The great thing to remember is that though our feelings come and go God's love for us does not."

—C.S. Lewis

"The great thing to remember is that though our feelings come and go God's love for us does not."
—C.S. Lewis

"The great thing to remember is that though our feelings come and go God's love for us does not."
—**C.S. Lewis**

"The great thing to remember is that though our feelings come and go God's love for us does not."

—C.S. Lewis

"The great thing to remember is that though our feelings come and go God's love for us does not."

—C.S. Lewis

"The great thing to remember is that though our feelings come and go God's love for us does not."
—**C.S. Lewis**

"The great thing to remember is that though our feelings come and go God's love for us does not."
—**C.S. Lewis**

"The great thing to remember is that though our feelings come and go God's love for us does not."

—**C.S. Lewis**

"The great thing to remember is that though our feelings come and go God's love for us does not."
—**C.S. Lewis**

_____

_____

_____

_____

_____

_____

_____

_____

_____

_____

_____

_____

_____

_____

_____

_____

_____

_____

_____

_____

"The great thing to remember is that though our feelings come and go God's love for us does not."

—C.S. Lewis

"The great thing to remember is that though our feelings come and go God's love for us does not."

—C.S. Lewis

"The great thing to remember is that though our feelings come and go God's love for us does not."

—C.S. Lewis

"The great thing to remember is that though our feelings come and go God's love for us does not."

—C.S. Lewis

"The great thing to remember is that though our feelings come and go God's love for us does not."
—**C.S. Lewis**

"The great thing to remember is that though our feelings come and go God's love for us does not."

—C.S. Lewis

"The great thing to remember is that though our feelings come and go God's love for us does not."

—C.S. Lewis

"The great thing to remember is that though our feelings come and go God's love for us does not."

—C.S. Lewis

_____

_____

_____

_____

_____

_____

_____

_____

_____

_____

_____

_____

_____

_____

_____

_____

_____

_____

_____

_____

_____

"The great thing to remember is that though our feelings come and go God's love for us does not."
—C.S. Lewis

"The great thing to remember is that though our feelings come and go God's love for us does not."
—**C.S. Lewis**

_____

_____

_____

_____

_____

_____

_____

_____

_____

_____

_____

_____

_____

_____

_____

_____

_____

_____

_____

_____

"The great thing to remember is that though our feelings come and go God's love for us does not."

—C.S. Lewis

"The great thing to remember is that though our feelings come and go God's love for us does not."

—C.S. Lewis

_____

_____

_____

_____

_____

_____

_____

_____

_____

_____

_____

_____

_____

_____

_____

_____

_____

_____

_____

_____

_____

_____

_____

"The great thing to remember is that though our feelings come and go God's love for us does not."

—C.S. Lewis

"The great thing to remember is that though our feelings come and go God's love for us does not."

—C.S. Lewis

"The great thing to remember is that though our feelings come and go God's love for us does not."
—**C.S. Lewis**

"The great thing to remember is that though our feelings come and go God's love for us does not."
—**C.S. Lewis**

"The great thing to remember is that though our feelings come and go God's love for us does not."

—C.S. Lewis

"The great thing to remember is that though our feelings come and go God's love for us does not."

—C.S. Lewis

"The great thing to remember is that though our feelings come and go God's love for us does not."
—C.S. Lewis

"The great thing to remember is that though our feelings come and go God's love for us does not."
—**C.S. Lewis**

"The great thing to remember is that though our feelings come and go God's love for us does not."

—C.S. Lewis

"Jesus Christ came not to condemn you but to save you, knowing your name, knowing all about you, knowing your weight right now, knowing your age, knowing what you do, knowing where you live, knowing what you ate for supper and what you will eat for breakfast, where you will sleep tonight, how much your clothing cost, who your parents were. He knows you individually as though there were not another person in the entire world. He died for you as certainly as if you had been the only lost one. He knows the worst about you and is the One who loves you the most.

If you are out of the fold and away from God, put your name in the words of John 3:16 and say, "Lord, it is I. I'm the cause and reason why Thou didst on earth come to die." That kind of positive, personal faith and a personal Redeemer is what saves you. If you will just rush in there, you do not have to know all the theology and all the right words. You can say, "I am the one He came to die for." Write it down in your heart and say, "Jesus, this is me—Thee and me," as though there were no others. Have that kind of personalized belief in a personal Lord and Savior."

— A.W. Tozer, *And He Dwelt Among Us: Teachings from the Gospel of John*

"The great thing to remember is that though our feelings come and go God's love for us does not."

—C.S. Lewis

REFERENCES

Carroll, L. (2006). Alice's adventures in Wonderland & through the looking-glass. New York, NY: Bantam Dell. (Original work published 1865)

Gilbert, E. (2006). Eat, pray, love: One woman's search for everything across italy, india and indonesia. New York, New York: Penguin Books.

Green, J. (2012). The fault in our stars. New York, New York: Dutton Books.

Henri J. M., N. (1986). Reaching out: The three movements of the spiritual life. Garden City, New York: Image Books.

Lewis, C. (1980). A Grief Observed. New York, New York: Seabury Press.

Manning, B. (2002). Abba's child: The cry of the heart for intimate belonging (Expanded ed.). Colorado Springs, Colorado: NavPress.

New American Standard Bible (Reference ed.). (1975). Chicago: Moody Press.

Rowling, J. (2000). Harry Potter and the goblet of fire. New York: Arthur A. Levine Books.

Smedes, L. (1984). Forgive and forget: Healing the hurts we don't deserve. San Francisco: Harper & Row.

Smedes, L. (1996). The art of forgiving: When you need to forgive and don't know how. Nashville, Tenn.: Moorings.

The Holy Bible: New international version, containing the Old Testament and the New Testament. (1978). Grand Rapids: Zondervan Bible.

The voice Bible: Step into the story of Scripture. (2012). Nashville, Tenn.: Thomas Nelson.

Tozer, A. (1961). The knowledge of the holy: The attributes of God, their meaning in the Christian life. New York: Harper & Row.

"The great thing to remember is that though our feelings come and go God's love for us does not."
—C.S. Lewis

Tozer, A., & Snyder, J. (2009). And He dwelt among us: Teachings from the gospel of John. Ventura, Calif.: Regal Books.

www.brenebrown.com

www.gungormusic.com

www.kimbramusic.com

OTHER GOODIES

www.bravelove.org

www.bigtoughgirl.com

www.lifeafterplacement.org

www.oyff.org

www.birthmombuds.com

"The great thing to remember is that though our feelings come and go God's love for us does not."

—**C.S. Lewis**

ACKNOWLEDGEMENTS

God. I am grateful for the suffering. You are a stunning groom; may I have this dance?

Matthew. I'm in love with you, but you will never be enough to satisfy my heart. Our kind of love is holier than thou. So glad we fell apart! Now we can live together.

My three children. You each are my teachers in your own ways. Being your mom is an overwhelming display of the goodness of God. I am thankful for the opportunity to parent each of you the best I can and I trust Jesus with the rest. I love you all!

Becky Bruns. You are so wise and have one of the most beautiful hearts I have ever witnessed. Knowing you is a privilege. Being your friend is an honor.

Beth James. There are few like you. I love your mother's heart and the fight in your eyes when someone is wronged. You love fiercely. It's inspiring!

Betty, Laura, Imprint Girls. What can I say? You get me. I get you. I'm sorry about that, but I'm thankful for each of you. You all are important to me. Much love!

Dan, Sallie, Kim. Good friends are hard to find, and for me, they are hard to keep. Thanks for loving this introvert. To Dan for connecting me to all of you via the world wide web (www.gestaltcreations.com). To Sallie for making me look beautiful in every photograph you have ever taken of me (www.sitesforyourlife.com). To Kim for helping me get here. You are the best kind of best friend--loyal, smart, and eager to offer advice. Thanks for reading all my crap!

Bethany Christian Services.
Thank you for giving me the opportunity to love these women without agenda.

City Church Charlotte.
I have to thank you all again. Al & Niki Hardy, Lindsay Rich, April Davis, Joy Mast, Holly Eskridge and few hundred others. Thank you for a safe place to sprout, for your love and guidance along the way, and for the cheerleading. Best community ever!

"The great thing to remember is that though our feelings come and go God's love for us does not."
—C.S. Lewis

"The great thing to remember is that though our feelings come and go God's love for us does not."

—C.S. Lewis

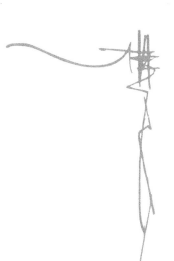

About the Author

Revealing You follows my first book, *Delivered: My Harrowing Journey as a Birthmother* (2012), a creative non-fiction work detailing my personal adoption experience. Since releasing *Delivered*, I have had the privilege of speaking about adoption both in public and private to audiences interested in the birthparent experience. I continue to blog on my website about God and adoption and my hope is that this journal will love you well. I wrote *Delivered* for me and *Revealing You* for you.

Other fun facts include: I am a wife, mother, birthmother, author extraordinaire, and Pregnancy Counselor for Bethany Christian Services in Little Rock, Arkansas, where I live with my aca-awesome husband and our two stellar children. I suffer from being a workaholic and habitually sticking my foot in my mouth. I have not-so-secret author crushes on C. S. Lewis, Brennan Manning, and Donald Miller. My favorite sport is Major League Baseball, but I will go hoarse yelling for the Oklahoma Sooners during football season. I have never met a stranger and have a knack for making others comfortable in uncomfortable situations. Above all, I love to laugh and make people laugh, and you may as well know that I am funnier when I stand up, which I am not doing as I type this. Apologies in advance!

www.michellethornebooks.com

"The great thing to remember is that though our feelings come and go God's love for us does not."

—C.S. Lewis

Made in the USA
Columbia, SC
21 June 2020